Bluebirds

and

FAITH

Best Wishes!
M. Gail Grant

M. Gail Grant

Dedication

Bluebirds and Faith is inspired by the greatest
man I have ever known, my daddy. He taught
me the most precious treasures in life are free;
we simply just need to look around us for
glimpses of God's grace. In these brief moments
of silent joy, hope thrives, for the soul is eternal.
The commandment is to simply — believe.

To my readers, I hope this poetry brings you
hope, faith, joy, and healing. Together, we are
much better than one.

Contents

Contents Continued . . .

Contents Continued . . .

Contents Continued . . .

Contents Continued . . .

Novelist

Prayers need no voice.

They simply live inside.

Each heart beats out the syllables

as God composes the words.

Holy Baptism

Emotion sweeps through me
as the water engulfs my sin.
The release of the red one's curse
litters the holy water's bin.

The life-force energy
courses through my pulsing veins,
as tears escape my eyes
in an attempt to release harbored pain.

Within my soul, I covet His promise.
No matter how dark
or dreadful my past,
God's Son forgives, as everlast
is His reign —
none can match.

I am born again,

and I simply have faith

that God's eternal blessings

will help me through each day.

The preacher declares

my sins are forgiven.

I rise from the water —

doubt is no longer misgiven.

Witnesses applaud,

as a new sister has joined

God's eternal family

as an innocent newborn.

All heads bow to pray

in sameness and rejoice,

for mortality's sins

are forgiven through Him.

Songs of a Bluebird

A bluebird's melody
sings songs of praise,
for the Son of God
was raised
from a makeshift grave.
Sin has found
its match
in the sacrificial lamb,
for He crushed
the evil one's curse
meant to destroy
heaven and earth.
Bluebirds remind us
of God's gift
of eternal grace.
Slow down and embrace,
letting go of the earthly race,
for the harmonious

musings of the

bluebird's song

will gently lead you away

from heartache and dismay.

Devil's Game

Anxiety and depression
are tools in his belt.

Numbness and pain
are part of his game.

Enjoyment he seeks
for the misery he reaps.

Darkness is his kiss,
while lost souls emanate
his sheer bliss.

Devastation and ruin
are his methods to instill
a sense of loss and surrender
to Lucifer's satanic will.

Recognize his futile tactics,
for nothing he does
can stand against God's grace
when we seek our Father's face.

One Step

Your last breath on earth leads to your first breath in heaven.

Remember this when you think one step can't lead to greatness.

We are only one step away from heaven.

Continue to put one foot in front of the other, but embrace each step with both meaning and purpose.

Together, each step brings you closer or further from your Heavenly Father.

Choose wisely.

Attributes

Humbleness and humility
are attributes to embrace,
for God's children, we are born,
and shall remain.

Heavenly fatherhood is forever
regardless of our chosen path.
Balancing love and disgust
must be arduous at best,
for humanity has grown,
putting morality to the test.

No matter how hurtful
our actions may be,
Father of all
will never
give up
on me.

Eternal Father

Loved by so many,

yet hidden from earthly sight.

Faithful presence known.

Holy Commandments

O ten commandments,
how to live eternally,
in honor of thee.

Magnificent One

Magnificent one

shoulders corruption for me.

Man's debt — no more.

Supreme Love

Love has many forms,
as Christ's own crucifixion —
the supreme one.

Communion

Breaking bread with wine
in remembrance of His deeds,
cleanses soul, indeed.

Merciful God

"Who am I?"
She asked in despair,
for the evil one
had broken her
beyond human repair.

You are mine,
He whispered,
for all that it's worth.
Your body and mind
were made from this earth.

"I am nothing,"
She replied,
"For I can't escape sin —
I have made so many mistakes that
I simply don't know where to begin."

Change is inevitable,
He replied with a fatherly grin.
Lift your heart, my sweet child,
as I dwell within.

"There is no more good,"
she surmised,
as the tears began to flow.
"I have nothing to give —
I have nothing worthy to show."

The evil one has tempted you.
Make no mistake —
turn your cheek the other way.
Embrace your future,
and let go of the past,
for nothing lives there
except the downcast.

She considered His words,
as her life flashed below.
Her feet were slipping
off the edge of a rocky plateau.

"Forgive me, dear Father,
I have lost my way.
I can't see my future —
I have gone too astray."

My Son paid the price
for all of earth's sin.
Lay down your worries,
and together, I will
help you live again.

His merciful words
transformed her nightmare,

as she felt His promises
fill the void in the stifling air.

She fell to her knees
and thanked the Lord
for his gift,
as Lucifer's deeds
were repented
with enduring fatigue.

God's forgiveness
ended the intrinsic rift.

Peace, my child,
is a reminder to seek Me.
You don't have to look far,
look to any binary star,
and you will see.

Choir

Vocal unison,

hymns old and new alike,

sing praise for the Son.

Church Pews

Wooden pews tonight,

brotherly worship in sight,

hushes anxious thoughts.

M. Gail Grant

Mosaic Visitor

Sunlit shapes dancing
through hand-carved stained glass windows.
God of light — here.

Washing Sin

Baptism redeems men
and women from early sins —
joined by holy gift.

Artistic Feathers

The blue from the sky
and the rust from the earth
majestically blend
with the artist's
soft touch
to paint
heavenly perfection
of each curve
with the brush.
God's beautiful creation
made from feathers
of love
fly inconspicuously
around us
in moments
of desperate need
— a gentle reminder
of the eternal creed.

Archangels

Archangels above
blow trumpets of gold with grace —
darkness erased.

Judas' Mission

Traitor by design.
Prophecy fulfilled in time —
Judas defines.

Noah's Gift

Noah, build your ark, please,

for waters are sure rising.

God will save us all.

Lion's Den

The lion's den awaits.

Armed with faith and God's grace,

a patient request.

Forbidden Wings

From heaven to hell
the dark angel has fallen,
burning flesh and soul.

Creation

Beginning of time —
His world immerged with mine,
O Father of blind.

Savior of Mine

Being a sinner,
man's holy walk through life is
paid by our savior.

Buried Sin

True love buries sin.

Our creator takes the fraught helm.

Forever, my friend.

Parenthood

Moments turn into days
and days turn into weeks.
Forever seems so astray.
I close my eyes
and dance in the memories
of your hand
holding mine,
as we skipped
to the playground
in the soft morning dew.
Through the eyes of a child
time seemed
to stand still,
as we focused
on swinging from the
monkey bars
with practiced skill.
I never realized

how such short moments

of childhood

would simply

instill

the bond of a

father and daughter

enjoying sweet pastimes,

while following

God's will.

As parents, we are blessed

with the task

of caring for God's own,

as children, we are born,

and quickly, we grow,

yet always known

as one of

His

own.

Angel Wings

White angel wings fan
from the corners of the earth
covering our sin.

Sad Eyes

Behind His sad eyes
betrayal smothered deep within
planned execution.

Victory Song

From high up above
to the valleys hidden low,
sweet victory sings.

Tick Tock

Tick tock from the clock.

Our messiah is returning.

Are you ready, King?

Beaten with Grace

In evil's dark face
lies the hidden seed of faith.
Brutally beaten.

Shepherd

By his shepherd staff,
watching over sinful lost flock,
souls will simply roam.

Thirsty

Starvation within,

endless hunger and wet thirst.

Through blood, God quenches.

Heaven's Bride

Heaven's bride will be
here for all humanity.
Ruling you and me.

Earth's Heartbeat

If all the earth

sang in harmonious pleasure,

consider the effects of brotherly love,

as nations become one.

If all the earth

sang in harmonious pleasure,

consider the effects of the unity of brethren,

as souls unite, defeating the evil one.

If all the earth

sang in harmonious pleasure,

consider the effects of forever,

as God's gift of grace

through His only Son

has paved the way

for wickedness

is

now,

undone.

Death

Frail and sickness, why?
All mighty Lord of so high,
please, no, don't die.

Red Sea

Parting the red sea,
saved Israelites from siege
as Moses helped free.

Rod and Staff

Great shepherd is He,

protecting his flock nightly,

using rod and staff.

Twelve Disciples

Twelve disciples meet.

For Jesus' teachings to greet

the lost souls who seek.

Lost Paradise

Jealousy and pride
is the fallen angel's greed.
Paradise is lost.

Bride's Covenant

The bride dressed in white
promises heaven above
for thee, she loves.

Emotional Glue

Kindness shapes the soul —
lengthening, bending, oh so.
Patience becomes glue.

My Father

Heavenly father
mercifully forgiving,
perfectly loving.

Broken

Shameful and broke,

He carries me through the storm.

Forgiven, Amen.

Circle of Life

Circle of life,

cycling over, yet again.

Death's curse is beaten.

M. Gail Grant

Bluebird's Reminder

The bluebird

sits on my windowsill

each day

softly reminding me

to live

God's way.

Starlight

Stars mimic wonder
of heavenly creation
for you and for me.

Just Ask

Why, sir, don't be shy,
God has commanded of you,
ask and receive.

Worldly Fame

Hollow wants bestowed
as riches and worldly fame
lead to anxious souls.

M. Gail Grant

Fueled by Fire

Evil thoughts birth flames

fueled most by greed's own name.

Burning smell — no gains.

A Bluebird's Gift

That moment in time
seems so surreal,
as I look back and think
about the glorious reveal.

*"Get a bluebird house, Bessie,
and hang it over there."*

"Where?"
I asked as the thought
had never occurred.
You see,
bird watching seemed a little absurd.

"On that tree, there, over there, you see?"

My eyes followed,
and sure enough,
to my disbelief,

stood a lone oak tree
on the edge of my property.

"But, dad, there is only one tree.
How do I know the bluebirds will find me?"

"Have faith, dear daughter, that's all
that you need."

Curious and unsure,
I couldn't figure out the need,
as surely bluebirds wouldn't find
this one skinny tree.

"Daddy, I know nothing about
caring for bluebirds,
but there's more,
if I hang the house,

I will need to ensure — worms and such,
it just won't work."

"Dear daughter, hang the house,
and you will see,
the bluebirds take care of their own,
and that's all they will need."

The seasons have blended together,
but his words remain with me.
Cancer took over with a mission
of its own, and I became lonely.

Your final breath took the life
out of me,
and through heartache and misery,
I chose not to believe.

God's rainbow promises

mercy and grace,

and all I remembered was the

glow on your face,

as you showed me not only

where,

but how

to believe.

Death may have separated us,

but the Holy One provides

the peace in forever

if we simply

arise.

I swallowed my tears.

My husband hung the bluebird

house for me,

following your guidance,

carefully in word and deed.

Desperate in hope

the size of

God's mustard seed,

I patiently waited to see

if bluebirds would find my

lonely oak tree.

Dear daddy,

you were right,

they frequently visit with me,

and they nest in the

faded bluebird house

hung on my tree.

The wisdom in your words
spoken so eloquently
feeds my faith
that you send them to visit
every spring.

I sit in the azalea garden
that now surrounds
this special tree,
as the bluebirds come and go
seemingly fear–free.

The lessons they have taught me
will likely be
what fuels my soul
for the rest of
eternity.

You knew you were dying,
yet shared humble blessings with me
through the wings of a bluebird
— so heavenly.

Never again will I doubt
how much God loves me,
for He gave us this special place
to give eternal thanks,
for His sacrifice of one
means the battle
for humanity is won.

Bluebird wings sent from
heaven above
continually announce your
presence
with sweet messages of love.

Together we remain
and together we will stand,
as God opens the pearly gates,
joining heaven and earth
in divine moments
of rebirth.

Victorious

Devilish wishes

destroyed as light takes the throne
of sweet victory.

M. Gail Grant

Christmas Eve

The eve of Christmas,

the defeated devil mourns.

The Lord's spirit — born!

Rainbow

God's sworn promises
dance in the heavenly light.
Rainbow colors bright.

M. Gail Grant

Neighbor

Loving my neighbor,

such a small price to be paid,

for heaven's home.

Evil Thirst

Evil hides from light,
savoring shadows' disguise
thirsty for my soul.

M. Gail Grant

Devil's Disguise

Disguised in the dark,

soul suffocating and mean,

luring innocent.

Eyes of a Child

Angelic of gifts,

His creation blossoms most

through child eyes wide.

Bundle of Love

Unearned gift to us,

baby bundle of love,

paid for all our sins.

Salvation

Deep and quite profound,

His sacrifice — eternal,

saving you and me.

Soulful Evolution

Have you ever noticed
how the soul
never seems to age?
The internal voice
inside of our head
speaks the same
from birth till death.
Evolution of self
underlines the maze,
as humanity seeks
for assurance
in heavenly ways.

Our King

Israel's newborn King,

nobility amongst thee,

suffered for small me.

Rescued

Beautifully,

charismatic and humble,

Jesus rescued me.

Covenant

Darkness has no hold

on our spiritual soul,

for the light of God's kingdom

represents an infinity of freedom.

When our earthly days

become treacherous

amidst the storm clouds and strife,

I will find solace in

His covenant

of

eternal

life.

Rebirth

No matter how hard we try,

humanity will always sin.

As a gracious Father,

our Lord has woven

forgiveness

and rebirth

into the fabric

of our

delicate skin.

True love knows no boundaries,

and His devotion to all

seeps in,

as life prepares

our soul

for a lifetime

with Him.

North Star

As our miracle was born,

the north star shone bright,

leading the way for humble shepherds,

wanting to experience the magnificent sight.

Lying in a manger,

amongst animals late at night,

Jesus Christ, our King,

delivered the world

from great plight.

Bluebird Wings

Bluebirds announce the arrival of spring,
for spiritual blessings renew with our King —
a gentle reminder that He is never far away.
Avoid the darkness and crippling dismay,
as proof of heaven resides in a bluebird's wing.

Earthly Parents

Mary and Joseph,

parents of the newborn King.

Holy blessed gift.

M. Gail Grant

Holy Trinity

Holy trinity —

Father, Son, and Holy Ghost,

here for all to see.

The Stable

Humble beginnings,
from stable manger to King
for eternity.

Musical Delight

Heaven and earth sing
glorious verses now ring
forever our King.

White Dove

White dove soaring high —

messenger of mountain tops.

Freedom for mankind.

Forgiveness

Learning to forgive yourself may be one of life's greatest challenges. If God can forgive our sins, who are we to question?

Just believe.

Renewal

Misery erased

from glorious redemption.
Renews our hope.

M. Gail Grant

Teardrops

Death is beaten down

as the sun rises eastward.

Teardrop stained face.

Reunion

Love beyond belief
sacrifice beyond measure
leaves weeping and blessed.

He Knows

You knew me,

before I was born.

You knew me,

as I crawled away.

You knew me,

when I walked the crooked path.

You knew me,

when I fell to my knees.

You knew me,

when I begged for mercy.

You knew me,

when I gave up.

You carried me,

when I needed you the most.

Betrayal

Almighty, my King!

Transcendent strength and course.

Betrayed and beaten.

Royal Birth

O three kings of night

treasure shining gold and bright

rejoice in His birth.

Remembrance

Holy remembrance —

He willfully died for me.

O, how can this be?

Thieves Acquitted

Thieves and murderers —
society's wretched adored
over our holy King.

His Child

Death lost the game.

Faith and grace have won my name

for His, I remain.

Jesus

He lived.

He died.

He saved.

Mentor in Sight

Feathers of blue,

breasts of burnt orange,

silhouette of beauty,

the body of a bluebird

manifests the essence

of calm

surrounded by God's

presence

with no sense of harm.

Learn from the stance

of a bluebird

in sight

as the wings expand

to help with

flight.

Open your heart

and

your mind

as the Lord
will provide
the wind for your wings
to propel you
high.

Virgin

From a virgin womb,

under the light of the moon,

King of kings is born.

Bethlehem

Oh, sweet Bethlehem,
host of eternity rings.
Music fills the air.

Martyr

Forever a king.

Divine martyr will become

tomorrow's hope.

Confiscated Sin

Through blood and soft tears,
divinity as a man
confiscated sin.

Rainbow of Love

F or God's promise remains

A s a vision on the horizon

I n full display of orchestrated color

T hat dance, and bend, and sway.

H old onto the faith!

Debt Paid

Tomorrow's great sin
was lovingly paid by Him
for ever–after.

Wooden Cross

Jesus, our savior,

nailed to the wooden pine cross.

Sacrificed for us.

Carpenter

Carpentry with hands,

brotherly love in His heart.

Jesus taught grace.

Darkness Canceled

Darkness has no reign,

for the light was born again,

saving our earned plight.

Sacrificial Lamb

Without God as man,

souls would treacherously burn.

Silenced by the Lamb.

Eve's Curse

Tree of knowledge,

the apple, man, and woman.

Division from God.

Heaven's Divide

As the bible says,

day and night divide the skies.

Pure darkness gone.

Goodbye

He never promised
life without hurt or unrest.
It is just a test.

Will His world or mine
survive the test of time?
Humanity, rise!

Flowers on the grave
symbolize memories old,
till we meet again.

Merciful Grace

Faith and hope by us —
heavenly merciful grace
leads to dwell with Him.

Praying Hands

Godly hands that pray

blesses the Father's children.

Raindrops of grace.

M. Gail Grant

Burning Soul

Hell leashes fury,

for the dark fallen angel,

lies to burn the soul.

Oneness

When you sit in stillness

and deafening silence,

the nothing you hear

is the knowledge

that you seek,

as the Holy One

lives inside

patiently waiting

for a moment

to

speak.

Disguised Angels

Sweet animals shared
their warm, cozy, humble home
to nestle our King.

Daylight

Morning dew, sweet kiss,

for dawn brings a new promise

of life without death.

No More

As the wind breaks through,

death humbly whispered adieu,

for the debt of humanity's sin

is paid by

Him.

Newborn

A newborn's first breath
begins the soul's lofty course
bridging the "I Am."

M. Gail Grant

Faith Heals

Broken hearts flow tears;
anger and pride steal your joy;
faith and hope will heal.

Glory to God

Bluebirds sing God's heavenly songs on earth —
do you listen?

Rise Above

Hate no more, my friend,

for jealousy will never win.

Protect your soul as though

humanity's greatest enemy

lives just below.

When anger and pride sets in,

remember, it is not

Him.

Turn your cheek,

and let the enemy reap

the burning flames

for

eternity.

I Believe

Eternal grace is

unearned — yet given to me.

Simply believe.

Devil's Delight

Horrid in

sight,

bound by

plight,

in an endless

fight,

leaves the enemy with

great delight.

Moses

Parting the red sea,
miracles witnessed by all.
Moses believed.

Starry Night

In Bethlehem born
one starry, cold, winter night.
Death's curse broken.

His Embrace

His arms open wide

as she cries in the dark night.

Father and His child.

Joseph

Gentleman, he walks

pulling the donkey at night,

for a stable manger

will foster the new life

sent to earth from heaven above

in a display

of

Fatherly love.

Golden Trumpet

Trumpets sound the news
eternity is the prize
singing praise ensues.

Rough Tides

Jesus,

He carried me

through the wicked storm of life.

Hatred and sin, the devil's gems,

withered.

The Journey

The white light in the tunnel
beckons me to come
and journey,
finally reaching the end.

As I run through the shadows,
I can't help but think
of the time unspent.

My tomorrow may not come
in the same space as yours,
but remember, my love,
we will one day meet again.

Life has so many distractions,
and I am as guilty as you,
of forgetting the meaning
of it all.

Embrace your humanness today,
and make it a plan that won't fail,
as avoiding the light in the tunnel
is futile to countervail.

Submissive Penance

S he whispered self-allegiance

I n an attempt to quell her pain.

N ever again would she own this shame.

M. Gail Grant

Graves of Death

Death mocks afflicted,
the horned–one likes to prey
on downtrodden graves.

Lucid Dream

I saw you
in my dreams tonight.
My heart feels warmth –
there was no fright.

I wondered where you
had been
since that fateful day,
when it all began.

I knew in the middle
of that crucial night,
as you awoke me,
before your long flight,
that the soul extends
beyond an internal vice.

We laughed and talked
just like before,
yet I knew in my dream,
it was because of our rapport.

Multidimensional in nature,
human consciousness transcends
to provide a safe space
in heavenly grace.

Short moments to capture —
a timeless love,
awaiting the sweet rapture.

By the Sea

As the heavens meet the sea,
His love rescues me
from dark moments of despair
when life feels beyond repair.

The ocean's coarse salt
cleanses my soul's mortal vault
until that symbolic day
that I leave this world on my way
to rest in eternal peace,
while heavenly angels release
bursts of ecstasy and joyous delight
in celebration of my ethereal flight.

The End

Author News

M. Gail Grant would like to thank her readers and kindly ask you to leave a review on GoodReads and the vendor from which you purchased your book if you feel inclined to do so! She is incredibly grateful for your feedback and thoughts for future readers.

Join our mailing list to receive periodic updates on new releases, sale information, and local author events:

MGailGrant.com
Facebook.com/MGailGrant
Twitter.com/MGailGrant
Instagram.com/MGailGrant